HOW TO STAND FIRM
IN TROUBLED TIMES

Dr. Rosie Rush

GLOBAL
PUBLISHING
SOLUTIONS

HOW TO STAND FIRM IN TROUBLED TIMES
by Dr. Rosie Rush
Published by Global Publishing Solutions, LLC
923 Fieldside Drive
Matteson, Illinois 60443
www.globalpublishingsolutions.com

Library of Congress Control Number:
2022914430
International Standard Book Number:
979-8-9853892-2-7
E-book International Standard Book Number:
979-8-9853892-1-0

Printed in the United States of America

DEDICATION

To Vivian, Ken and Beverly, and Terry and Yolanda. To my precious grandchildren: Jana, Genesis, Tre' Nolan, Trennon, Yani, and Aria. To the greatest and most supportive and caring family who has made my life so rich and blessed. To my Mom, Dad, and George and Rosie Clark, for the values you instilled in me as a child.

To my goddaughters, Stephanie and Sukia, and my godson Craig Hale.

CONTENTS

CHAPTER ONE

HOW TO STAND FIRM IN TROUBLED TIMES

Subject: "Standing Firm in Troubled Times"

THE DEFINITION OF THE WORD FIRM[1]

1. Having a solid, almost unyielding surface or structure.
2. Strongly felt and unlikely to change.

Several definitions were given for the word firm; we chose to use the adverb form of the word firm; it says standing firm in a determined manner.

Often, we must take a stand in situations and circumstances, and sometimes our stand is weak intentionally, sometimes weak not intentionally. My

---

[1] https://www.oed.com

example of an intentionally weak stance when my grandkids were young, if they did not respond immediately to my call to join me on the lower level of the house. After repeated requests for them to come down had been ignored, I'd yell, "Don't let me have to come up there." It was just a bluff. I had no intention of climbing those stairs. But since they didn't know that it was a bluff, I got the desired results. That's intentionally weak. However, standing firm and weak unintentionally is when you allow things to get out of control before you act on them, or you took a firm stance too late (you waited until your son or daughter got to be teenagers before you started to discipline them). So, now you have trouble. Therefore, we find that if we are going to be able to stand firm in troubled times, we must decide when there is no trouble, the stance that we will take when trouble comes. We can then adhere to the advice of Paul to the Corinthians:

1 CORINTHIANS 15:58 Therefore, my beloved brethren, be ye steadfast, unmovable, always abounding in the work of the Lord, forasmuch as ye know that your labour is not in vain in the Lord. In our family and everyday lives, we must be steadfast.

Decisions are hard to make in the midst of problems, which is why some people make their funeral arrangements while they are healthy and happy, so the family won't be taken advantage of in their grief. In this life, it's not if troubles come, it's when troubles come, as we see in the book of Job.

CHAPTER TWO

JOB 14:1 Job said, "that a man that is born of a woman is of few days and full of trouble." So, in each of our lives trouble will come, it's just a matter of when—not if. So, let's take a good look at trouble. Trouble can take on many forms. Trouble is defined as: to disturb the mental calm and contentment of; worry, distress, agitate, to cause bodily pain, discomfort, or disorder, to afflict.[2] As you can easily see, no one will get through life without incurring trouble in some of these categories. I read a cliché that said, "into each life some rain must fall," **but this is ridiculous**, and perhaps many have felt that way about the troubles of life.

But there is one bright side to trouble, it doesn't last always. We can look at it as just a test that prepares us for the next level in life's destiny. As we go through trouble, it is always good to keep in mind that winners don't quit,

---

[2] https://www.dictionary.com/browse/troubled

and quitters don't win. We must be assured that we are winners. Winners never brag or boast, but they always put forth their best effort.

One consolation of standing firm is knowing that what you are going through has an expiration date. It will come to an end here or there. So, what Paul in the book of Ephesian tells us how to prepare for our standing.

CHAPTER THREE

EPHESIANS 6:10-13 ¹⁰ Finally my brethren, be strong in the Lord, and in the power of his might. ¹¹ Put on the whole armor of God that ye may be able to stand against the wiles of the devil. ¹² for we wrestle not against flesh and blood, but against principalities, against powers, against the rulers of the darkness of this world, against spiritual wickedness in high places. ¹³ Wherefore take unto you the whole armor of God that ye may be able to withstand in the evil day, and having done all, to stand. ¹⁴ Stand therefore, having your loins girt about with truth, and having on the breastplate of righteousness; ¹⁵ And your feet shod with the preparation of the gospel of peace; ¹⁶ Above all, taking the shield of faith, wherewith ye shall be able to quench all the fiery darts of the wicked. ¹⁷ And take the helmet of salvation, and the sword of the Spirit, which is the word of God: ¹⁸ Praying always with all prayer and supplication in the Spirit, and watching thereunto with all perseverance and supplication for all saints.

Finally! After you have done all you know to do, you still stand. But how? My brethren, be strong in the Lord, not in yourself, but in the power of His might and of His Strength. Now he also tells us how to do that. Paul says that we must put on the whole armor. No doubt some of the armor in the natural as they prepared for battle was uncomfortable, but if they wanted to be protected in the fight, they nevertheless had to put it on. It was for their protection.

Getting committed to God and being faithful is not an easy task. It takes time, perseverance, willingness, determination, truthfulness, and integrity. For we must seek Him with our whole heart, learn of Him, get to know Him, love and trust Him, rely totally on Him, and then He enables us to stand with the power of His might dressed in the whole Armor. At no time are we to be without the full armor of God, because Satan is always lurking to see what part of our mind is left uncovered. His battle begins in the mind. It is an awesome thing to always have a clear conscience, knowing that you are following the word of truth, being fair in every situation toward others, and walking in love.

After all, the Bible tells us that faith worketh by love. So, there are some requirements to standing firm in troubled times. Let us keep in mind that every stance we take must be grounded on the word of God, for Jesus is the solid rock. All other grounds regardless of the names, wealth, fame, or fortune are all sinking sand.

As Paul talks about the breastplate of righteousness, which is our right standing in Christ or our positional righteousness. Our actions should also be in line with our positional righteousness. If we are the King's kid, we should act like King's kids, by walking according to His word, or else we give the King a bad reputation, both natural and spiritual. The reason for this is so that the devil will not be able to have a legitimate reason to accuse us or defeat us when we are in right standing with the Lord. It is the righteousness of Christ that assures our salvation.

It is impossible to stand without the shoes of the gospel. We must know, believe in, trust. and rely on the word of

God, which are the shoes of the gospel. Paul tells us what the gospel is in **1 CORINTHIANS 15:1-4**.

CHAPTER FOUR

1 CORINTHIANS 15:1-4

Moreover, brethren, I declare unto you the gospel which I preached unto you, which also ye have received, and wherein ye stand; ² by which also ye are saved, if ye keep in memory what I preached unto you, unless ye have believed in vain.

³ For I delivered unto you first of all that which I also received, how that Christ died for our sins according to the scriptures; ⁴ And that he was buried, and that he rose again the third day according to the scriptures:

Notice! The brethren were standing on the Gospel they had heard and had received. They heard it, they received it, and now they can stand firm on what they heard. Their feet are shod with the preparation of the Gospel They had to believe that Christ died, rose again—They knew that the resurrection was the most important part of the message, because a dead Christ cannot save anybody.

Paul's readers had received the Word, trusted Christ, and been saved and were now standing firm on that Word as the assurance of their salvation.

CHAPTER FIVE

ROMANS 10:17 "So then faith cometh by hearing, and hearing by the word of God." The Gospel is the most important message to the church and for the church to proclaim to others. There may be a lot of things we can stand on, but in the end, they are just sinking sand. Faith in God is the only sure foundation. Faith comes from the word of God. Prayers do not produce faith. The hearing of the word and acting on what you hear is the only way to increase faith.

CHAPTER SIX

This is what separates Our Christianity from all others. It is found in **JOHN 3:16**.

¹⁶ For God so loved the world that he gave his only begotten Son, that whosoever believeth in him should not perish, but have everlasting life.

The truth is that Jesus rose from the dead. He died, He was buried, and He rose again. Therefore, when we place our hope, our trust, and our faith in Him, we can stand firm. He did all this for us.

This enables us to face the many tests, trials, and troubles that come into our lives—even the ones we bring on ourselves.

As you read the Bible, you can see all the problems that David encountered that he brought on himself; His son

Amnon raped his sister Tamar, and Amnon was later killed by her brother Absalom. David at one point had to flee for his life from his own son Absalom, who also tried to dethrone him. But David stood firm in spite of his troubles, even if he did bring them on himself.

Standing firm in troubled times requires a made-up mind. You have to believe it. I will not yield or compromise, but I will trust God in every situation no matter what. Now when we really look at our strength that is "zilch," what choice do we have but to trust God? Where else can we get real help from? Even the friends and family who are there to support us are there because of the grace and direction from God.

Those who trust in God are not easily moved by negative circumstances or negative opinions of others. They know in whom they can truly rely on.

It is impossible to stand firm in troubled times unless you have a relationship with Jesus. Though I was a musician for many years and familiar with so many songs that conveyed so many different messages, trying to stand without God on your side would be like the words of this song, sometimes up, and sometimes down, sometimes level to the ground. Well, you would really be always level to the ground.

Then, there is another song that says, "Order my steps in your word." When your steps are ordered by God, you can stand firm. The Bible says that the steps of a good man are ordered by the Lord.

CHAPTER SEVEN

PSALMS 37:23-24; [23] The steps of a good man are ordered by the Lord: and he delighteth in his way. [24] Though he falls, he shall not be utterly cast down: for the Lord upholdeth him with his hand.

Unless we have some direction for our lives, we can and will make major mistakes, because our ways seem right. It is always easy to go with the flow. Most time, the flow is flowing down stream and can gather such strong momentum before you even realize that you have drifted into a whirlpool or a cesspool. Standing firm will cause you to test the waters. Is it still? Is it refreshing? Is it relaxing? Does it help or aid my progress?

Standing firm in troubled times will bring you to the conclusion that this journey is between you and God. No matter how many well-wishers, some would if they could, and some could if they would. But the bottom line is that it is up to you to stand firm with your faith in God.

CHAPTER EIGHT

One of my favorite scriptures is **PROVERBS 3:5-6**, [5] Trust in the Lord with all thine heart; and lean not unto thine own understanding. [6] In all thy ways acknowledge him, and he shall direct thy paths. This is a word that you can stand firm on. We come to realize that our understanding is faulty, but God makes no mistakes. He knows the path that we would take if left to ourselves, and He knows the path that He has designed for our lives. As we acknowledge Him, He orders our steps in the path He has designed for us.

CHAPTER NINE

We find that path by studying His word. **PSALMS 119:105** Thy word is a lamp unto my feet and a light unto my path. It enables you to see where you are standing and also where you are stepping, as you walk according to God's word. When growing up in the South, my family owned 90 acres of land. We could walk in many directions. Often times we would walk at night, but we had to carry a lantern to make sure that we were taking the correct path leading home. I was about 3 or 4 years old, but I still remember my great grandmother visiting some of her relatives. On her way home late in the evening, she got caught in a storm of rain and wind and never made it home because she could not see her way. She lost her way home and died in the storm.

Do you ever wonder why we have storms, or trials and tribulations? Is it just to interrupt a smooth sailing life? Or is it to keep us from living what we might call the "good live"—whatever that is. No! There are reasons for every trial and every test that we go through, and they are for our own good'

CHAPTER TEN

1 PETER 4:12-13

¹² Beloved, think it not strange concerning the fiery trial, which is to try you, as though some strange thing happened unto you: ¹³ but rejoice, inasmuch as ye are partakers of Christ's sufferings; that, when his glory shall be revealed, ye may be glad also with exceeding joy.

In other words, what Peter is saying is nothing new. This has been happening all along, and as we study church history and hear of the false accusations and the harsh treatment of the Saints while they stood in faith, or even when we read Hebrews Chapter eleven and get just a brief summary of what they suffered but stood firm in troubled times.

Troubled times are not to show God how strong we are, but it is for us to see for ourselves how weak we are and how much we need to depend completely on Him. That is the only way we can stand firm in troubled times. Only then can we look back and smile with a heart of thanksgiving as we realize that it was for our own good and that God has caused us to triumph through Him in this test. That victory will enable us to have confidence that God will do it again in the next encounter, and the next and the next, and on and on. It will also increase our faith in our ability to rely on his choice of ways that He intervenes in our struggles. He cannot be boxed in. It is not our business to figure out how, when, or where he will work on our behalf, but just trust and know that he will.

CHAPTER ELEVEN

James says in

JAMES 1:2-4

² My brethren, count it all joy when ye fall into diver's temptations; ³ knowing this, that the trying of your faith worketh patience. ⁴ But let patience have her perfect work, that ye may be perfect and entire, wanting nothing.

Our outlook determines our outcome, and our attitude determines our actions. God tells us to expect trials. It is not "if you fall into various tastings" but "when you fall into various tastings." The believer who expects his Christian life to be easy is in for a shock. Jesus warned His disciples, "In the world ye shall have tribulation." Notice he did say when you fall into temptation, and he did not say when you yield to temptation. There is a difference.

CHAPTER TWELVE

JOHN 16:33

[33] These things I have spoken unto you, that in me ye might have peace. In the world ye shall have tribulation: (affliction, trials, testing) but be of good cheer; I have overcome the world. We are overcomers in Him.

Because we are God's "scattered people" and not God's "sheltered people," we must experience trials. We cannot always expect everything to go our way. Some trials come simply because we are human or because of sickness, accidents, disappointments, or some other tragedies. Other trials come because we are Christians.

CHAPTER THIRTEEN

Peter emphasizes this in his first letter: (**1 PETER 4:12**) "Beloved, think it not strange concerning the fiery trial which is to try you, as though some strange thing happened unto you" Satan fights us, the world opposes us, and this makes for a life of battles. But guess what? We win if we stand firm. We also have to remember that the battle is not ours, it is the Lord's, but we do have to show up. But not as if we are on the "love boat" but on a battleship ready for battle.

CHAPTER FOURTEEN

We have been given power over all the works of the enemy, according to

LUKE 10:19 Behold, I give unto you power to tread on serpents and scorpions, and over all the power of the enemy: and nothing shall by any means hurt you. Although we will go through some things, but we do not think that it is strange, for we have been given the power and we use the authority that have been given to us. We then know that no weapon formed against us shall prosper. Simply because we have the word of God to stand on, and He has given His angel charge over us to keep us in all our ways.

Angels do exist. They are sent to minister for those who shall be heirs of salvation.

CHAPTER FIFTEEN

HEBREWS 1:14

[14] Are they not all ministering spirits, sent forth to minister for them who shall be heirs of salvation?

While visiting a college campus with one of my girls, the person that was in the office said that the office was closed until a certain time of the day. We were invited to just sit outside of the office and wait. In the meantime, this person came and sat down beside us and began to give us information concerning the school that convinced me to enroll my daughter in that school, in spite of the cost. It was not that he was promoting the school "per se" but just giving factual information. If I had not been given that information, I would have returned home without enrolling her. After my daughter spent four and a half years and graduated from that college, she never saw that person, and no one had ever heard of that person. Did God just send that angel to help me make the right decision? I believe He did so that I could stand firm in my faith that God would order my steps and provide what we needed for that school. It was the right decision.

As we determine to stand firm, God supplies all the needs that we have. Let's look at the morning after the crucifixion.

CHAPTER SIXTEEN

MARK 16:1-4

[1] And when the Sabbath was past, Mary Magdalene, and Mary the mother of James, and Salome, had bought sweet spices that they might come and anoint him. [2] And very early in the morning the first day of the week, they came unto the Sepulcher at the rising of the sun. [3] And they said among themselves, who shall roll us away the stone from the door of the sepulcher? [4] And when they looked, they saw that the stone was rolled away: for it was very great.

These women went to take care of the business of anointing Jesus' body with the sweet spices they had bought. They knew that the stone was there because they asked the question, who is going to roll away the stone for us? But I noticed they never stopped to say oh well, the stone is too large, we might as well wait and see if someone else will go and move it, or we could just cancel our trip, go get a refund on our spices, and call it a day. NO! They were standing fast on their commitment to go and anoint his body, and as they continued, they saw that the stone was already rolled away for them. You cannot back up once you have made a decision to stand firm on God's word, or you will become a double-minded man, who is unstable in all his ways, and will receive nothing from God according to James.

CHAPTER SEVENTEEN

JAMES 1:6-8

[6] But when he asks, he must believe and not doubt, because he who doubts is like a wave of the sea, blown and tossed by the wind. [7] That man should not think he will receive anything from the Lord; [8] he is a double-minded man, unstable in all he does. I heard a phrase once that said, "you are not what you think you are, but you are what you think." Now that can be a vast difference. In other words, we must let God be the final authority on what we really need. I like to use **PROVERBS 3:5-6** on any decision that I have to make that is not specifically outlined in the word of God. Yes. I do make an effort to accomplish the things I desire, but God has my permission to block it if it's not

his will. Every time that happens, I am able to look back and say thank you Lord, because that would not have been the right decision.

CHAPTER EIGHTEEN

PROVERBS 23:7

[7] For as he thinketh in his heart, so is he: Eat and drink, saith he to thee; but his heart is not with thee. In this case with his mouth, he is saying you are welcome to eat and drink. But in his heart, he could be thinking about how costly the food is that you are eating, or he could be cheap or stingy. In reality, you are not really welcome to his food.

Remember the advertisement that says, "if only people would say what they mean"? Truth spoken in love would be of great help when it is received as given. God has given us the gift of the spirit of discernment. So, we discern, and we keep standing firm by walking in love.

CHAPTER NINETEEN

GALATIANS 6:1

Brethren, if a man be overtaken in a fault, ye which are spiritual, restore such a one in the spirit of meekness; considering thyself, lest thou also be tempted. No man is an island. You cannot stand firm alone. Some people are put on the island to help you, and you are put on the island to help someone else. All of our work should be done in love and in the spirit of meekness as the scripture says, "considering thyself." If you have noticed the hand gesture as you point a finger at someone else, three fingers are pointing back at you. That makes us realize that, except for the grace of God, we could be the ones overtaken in the fault. Therefore, we are to treat others as we want to be treated. The golden rule says "Do unto others as you would have them do unto you"—not do unto others before they do unto you.

As we look at those that have gone before us and who left us a model of how to stand firm, we must first notice that they stood on their faith, because the word said without faith it is impossible to please God.

CHAPTER TWENTY

HEBREWS 11:6-13

[6] But without faith it is impossible to please him: for he that cometh to God must believe that he is, and that he is a rewarder of them that diligently seek him.

[7] By faith Noah, being warned of God of things not seen as yet, moved with fear, prepared an ark to the saving of his house; by which he condemned the world, and became heir of the righteousness which is by faith.

[8] By faith Abraham, when he was called to go out into a place which he should after receive for an inheritance, obeyed; and he went out, not knowing whither he went.

⁹ By faith he sojourned in the land of promise, as in a strange country, dwelling in tabernacles with Isaac and Jacob, the heirs with him of the same promise:

¹⁰ For he looked for a city which hath foundations, whose builder and maker is God.

¹¹ Through faith also Sara herself received strength to conceive seed, and was delivered of a child when she was past age, because she judged him faithful who had promised.

¹² Therefore sprang there even of one, and him as good as dead, so many as the stars of the sky in multitude, and as the sand which is by the sea shore innumerable.

¹³ These all died in faith, not having received the promises, but having seen them afar off, and were persuaded of them, and embraced them, and confessed that they were strangers and pilgrims on the earth.

First, we notice that they knew that they would be rewarded, because they were seeking the will of God. We know that he is a rewarder, that's how and why we can stand firm. Now let's look at the obedience of Noah. He kept building the ark against all odds. Can you visualize the stamina it took to continue working while others could have probably been mocking or being sarcastic? But he stood firm and was rewarded in the end with the saving of his family and the beginning of a new world after the flood.

Abraham had to stand firm on his conviction in order to just get up and go without knowing where he was going. Standing firm takes obedience. His obedience was rewarded by the promise of God to him, his natural seed, and his faith seed recipients that includes us. Let's give Sarah credit for she received the strength to bring forth a son in her old age. All this happen because they believed God and stood firm on his word. Now the amazing thing to me about Abraham is that after he fathered Isaac and Sarah had died, he remarried and had 6 more children according to **GENESIS 25:1.**

GENESIS 25:1-7

[1] Then again Abraham took a wife, and her name was Keturah. [2] And she bares him Zimran, and Jokshan, and Medan, and Midian, and Ishbak, and Shuah.

[3] And Jokshan begat Sheba, and Dedan. And the sons of Dedan were Asshurim, and Letushim, and Leummim.

[4] And the sons of Midian; Ephah, and Epher, and Hanoch, and Abida, and Eldaah. All these were the children of Keturah.

[5] And Abraham gave all that he had unto Isaac.

⁶ But unto the sons of the concubines, which Abraham had, Abraham gave gifts, and sent them away from Isaac his son, while he yet lived, eastward, unto the east country.

⁷ And these are the days of the years of Abraham's life which he lived, a hundred threescore and fifteen years. When God said to Abraham that I will make of thee a great nation, all the nation of the earth would be blessed. He kept his word.

GENESIS 12:3

³ And I will bless them that bless thee, and curse him that curseth thee: and in thee shall all families of the earth be blessed (Abraham seed have covered the earth, both naturally and spiritually).

CHAPTER TWENTY-ONE

GALATIANS 3:8

[8] And the scripture, foreseeing that God would justify the heathen through faith, preached before the gospel unto Abraham, saying, in thee shall all nations be blessed (Thanks be to God that we get to be included through Jesus Christ who shed his blood for us on the cross of Calvary delivered us from the curse. Hallelujah!)

We received the same gospel that Paul described in **1 CORINTHIANS 15:4**. We receive it by confessing with our mouth and believing in our heart that God has raised Jesus from the dead.

CHAPTER TWENTY-TWO

ROMANS 10:9-13

[9] That if thou shalt confess with thy mouth the Lord Jesus, and shalt believe in thine heart that God hath raised him from the dead, thou shalt be saved.

[10] For with the heart man believeth unto righteousness; and with the mouth confession is made unto salvation.

[11] For the scripture saith, whosoever believeth on him shall not be ashamed.

[12] For there is no difference between the Jew and the Greek: for the same Lord over all is rich unto all that call upon him

[13] For whosoever shall call upon the name of the Lord shall be saved.

The same rules apply to everyone and anyone! Isn't that good news. This is the establishment of a solid foundation. Everything else is faulty. You have probably heard of a lot of other attempts. The Bible said that there is no other name under Heaven given among men whereby we must be saved. And let me add here also about the things we pray for from the Lord. We must confess them with our mouth and believe that we receive them in order to possess them. As you remember, death and life are in the power of the tongue. If you speak life, you get life. If you speak death, you get death. Therefore, our minds should be renewed by the word of God so that the things we speak will be in line with God's word because the scripture says that God hastens to perform his word. If we speak it, he will perform it. **His words**, not just something that we say, our words must be in line with His word.

CHAPTER TWENTY-THREE

ACTS 4:5-14

⁵ And it came to pass on the morrow, that their rulers, and elders, and scribes,

⁶ And Annas the high priest, and Caiaphas, and John, and Alexander, and as many as were of the kindred of the high priest, were gathered together at Jerusalem.

⁷ And when they had set them in the midst, they asked, by what power, or by what name, have ye done this?

⁸ Then Peter, filled with the Holy Ghost, said unto them, Ye rulers of the people, and elders of Israel,

⁹ If we this day be examined of the good deed done to the impotent man, by what means he is made whole;

¹⁰ Be it known unto you all, and to all the people of Israel, that by the name of Jesus Christ of Nazareth, whom

ye crucified, whom God raised from the dead, even by him doth this man stands here before you whole.

11 This is the stone which was set at naught of you builders, which is become the head of the corner.

12 Neither is there salvation in any other: for there is none other name under heaven given among men, whereby we must be saved.

When Jesus went to the cross, he paid the price for all the benefits that have been made available to us. It is because of His blood shed on the cross that we obtain salvation. Salvation describes the full range of divine activity in physical and spiritual deliverance, both past, present, and future.

Now if you notice, the man was standing there whole, which indicated that he was healed from his infirmities, his sin, and his poverty. The curse was broken off his life.

Afterward, he was able to stand firm physically and spiritually.

One of my favorite Bible characters in the Old Testament is Daniel. As we read the book of Daniel, we notice that as he was taken captive in Babylon. He resolved from the beginning that he would not compromise his stance on what he believed. His mind was made up; therefore, he did not have to try and figure out his position as he went along. He determined to stay true to God at all costs, and as a result, God stayed true to him. And the same applied to the three Hebrew boys, who were Daniel's companions. They did not wait until the fiery furnace was looming in their sight to make up their mind, they had already made the decision to stay with God.

As we read that story in the book of Daniel about the three Hebrew boys, a good question for each of us to ask ourselves is: will I bow, will I burn, or will I survive? Their answer to the king was, "we will not "bow." This was their final answer.

Finally, to stand firm in time of trouble, you must be grounded and anchored in Jesus. To be anchored in Jesus is to be anchored in his word.

CHAPTER TWENTY-FOUR

JOHN 1:1

¹ In the beginning was the Word, and the Word was with God, and the Word was God.

JOHN 1:14

¹⁴ And the Word was made flesh, and dwelt among us, (and we beheld his glory, the glory as of the only begotten of the Father,) full of grace and truth. We can- not be anchored in God without being anchored in His word. As we continue in Him and His word remains in us, we are winners. Jesus has already won the battle for us; we just have to recognize that and continue to the end. It becomes easier when you already know the outcome.

I have grandchildren that play basketball in another state. I love watching them play, but I cannot live stream while they are playing. But once the game is over and the winner has been determined, I can watch the game play by play, which is great because there is no pressure of being anxious hoping that they win. After all, I already know the outcome. THEY ARE WINNERS (at least the ones I choose to watch).

So, it is when we stand firm that we already know the outcome. The battle has already been won by Jesus at the cross of Calvary. He defeated every foe. Therefore, when Satan and his demonic forces raise their ugly heads, we have the power to let them know that we know that they are already defeated, and we will remain standing firm until we receive the victory of the crown that is laid up for us.

If you have not received the Lord as your savior and you are ready to take a firm stand for Him, please pray this simple prayer and receive him into your life. You will never regret it.

PRAY THIS PRAYER:

Dear Lord in the Name of Jesus, your word says whosoever shall call on the name of the Lord shall be saved (Romans 10:13). I call upon you today from the depths of my heart, confessing that I am a sinner and need your saving grace. Your word said that if I confess with my mouth the Lord Jesus, and if I believe in my heart that God has raised Him (Jesus) from the dead, I will be saved. I believe in my heart, and I confess Jesus as my Lord.

Thank you, Jesus, that I am now saved.

Find a Church where the word is being taught, and you can have fellowship with other saints and grow in the Lord.

ABOUT THE AUTHOR

Evangelist Dr. Rosie Rush, a born-again woman of God who ministers under the anointing and delights in doing God's will, has ministered throughout many states, speaking for congregations, conferences, and workshops. She served as interim pastor for in state and out of state ministry.

Evangelist Dr. Rosie Rush is an associate minister of Christian Valley M. B. Church. She has also served as assistant pastor to Senior Saint Outreach Church. Both churches are located in the Chicagoland Area. She has served as the Academic Dean of the Living Word Outreach Full Gospel College and School of Ministry in Chicago Heights, Illinois and on the teaching staff.

Evangelist Rush holds an Associate Degree in Biblical Studies, a Bachelor's degree in Theology, a Master's Degree in Theological Studies, and a Doctorate of Ministry.

Evangelist Dr. Rush has been in the teaching ministry for more than 35 years in various capacities.

She is a member of Phi Beta Kappa. She served on the executive board of the former RAY Foundation.

She is also a representative for the 3rd ward coalition of Chicago Heights.

HOW TO STAND FIRM IN TROUBLED TIMES

67

www.ingramcontent.com/pod-product-compliance
Lightning Source LLC
Chambersburg PA
CBHW060349130626
46553CB00003B/1148